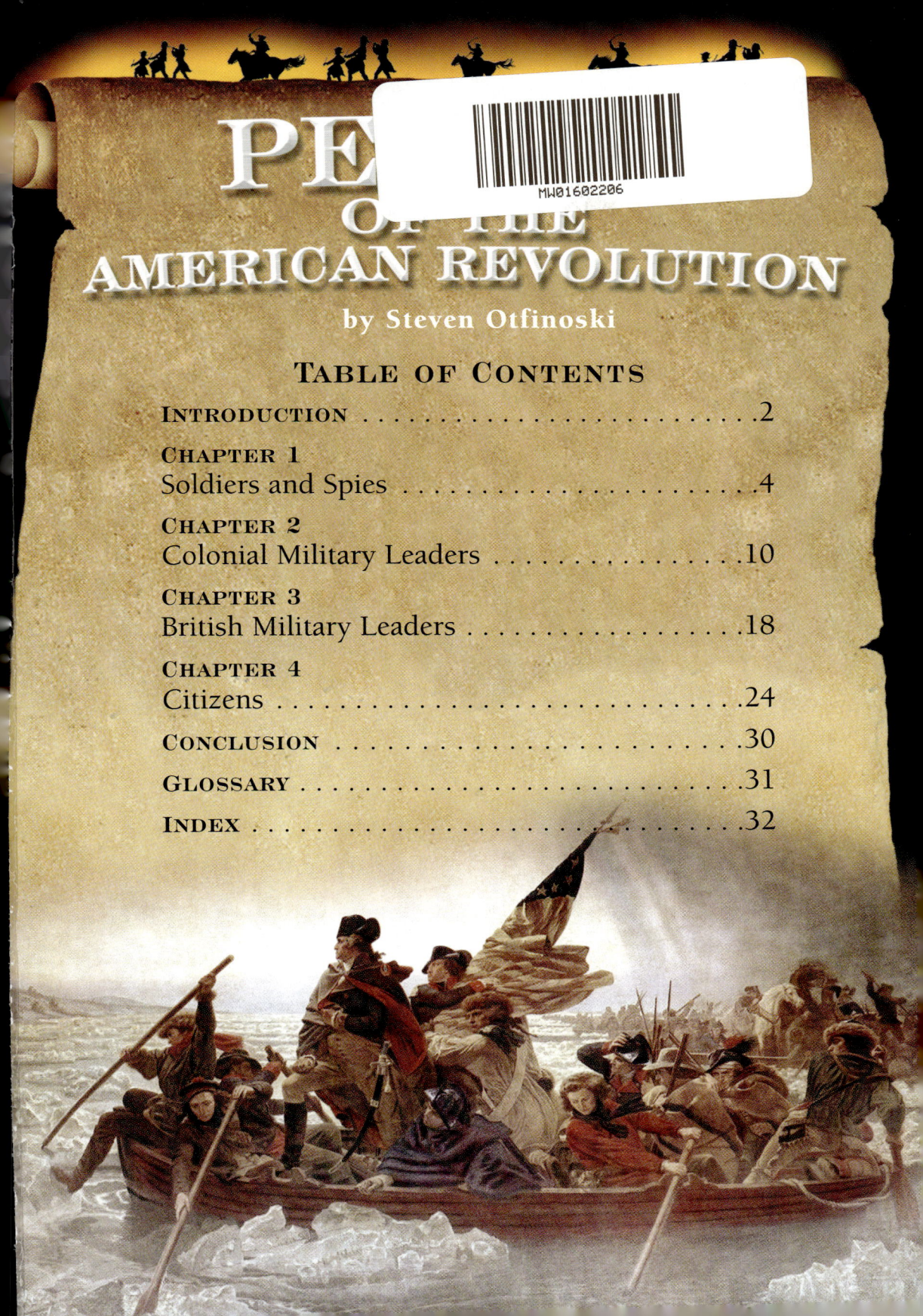

PE
OF THE
AMERICAN REVOLUTION
by Steven Otfinoski

TABLE OF CONTENTS

INTRODUCTION

The American Revolution lasted eight years. When it started, no one thought the colonists could win. When it ended, the British were defeated. The United States of America was a new nation.

People came together to fight for freedom. What kind of people helped win the American Revolution?

HISTORICAL PERSPECTIVE

According to leader John Adams, only a third of all colonists wanted freedom from the British. They were called **Patriots**. Another third of the colonists supported the king of England. They were called **Loyalists**. The rest did not choose sides. Even today, people do not agree with the same idea when it comes to war.

▲ This statue of a "Minuteman" stands for the fighting spirit of the American Revolution. It is in a park in Boston.

▲ The British marched to Concord on April 19, 1775, to destroy Patriot military supplies.

Some were rich and well educated. Others were poor and couldn't read.

Some fought as soldiers. Others gathered information on the British. These were spies. Some fought with words. They urged on other colonists with speeches, **pamphlets** (PAM-fluts), and even plays.

All their efforts helped the **Patriots** (PAY-tree-uts) fight on. In the end, they led their nation to victory.

In these pages, you will meet some people of the American Revolution. Ten of them fought on the Patriot side. Three fought on the British side.

SOLDIERS AND SPIES

Nathan Hale

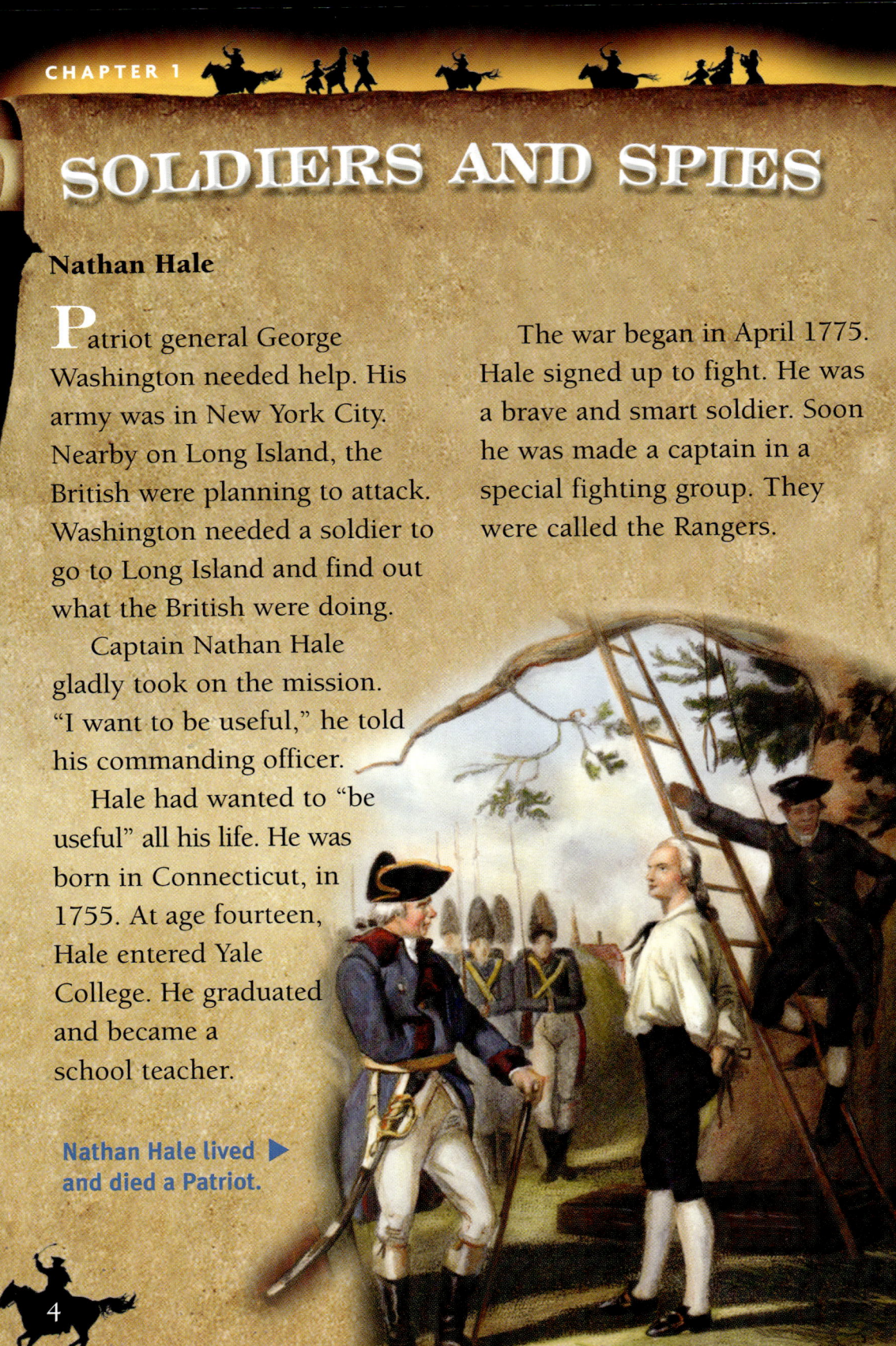

Patriot general George Washington needed help. His army was in New York City. Nearby on Long Island, the British were planning to attack. Washington needed a soldier to go to Long Island and find out what the British were doing.

Captain Nathan Hale gladly took on the mission. "I want to be useful," he told his commanding officer.

Hale had wanted to "be useful" all his life. He was born in Connecticut, in 1755. At age fourteen, Hale entered Yale College. He graduated and became a school teacher.

The war began in April 1775. Hale signed up to fight. He was a brave and smart soldier. Soon he was made a captain in a special fighting group. They were called the Rangers.

Nathan Hale lived ▶ and died a Patriot.

"I only regret that I have but one life to lose for my country."
– Nathan Hale

To spy on the British, Hale disguised himself as a teacher. He pretended to be a Loyalist. He learned all he could about the British plans. He started back to the Patriot side, but British soldiers stopped him. They quickly found out that he was a spy. Some people say Hale's cousin was a Loyalist who reported him to the British soldiers.

Hale was brought before British General William Howe. He ordered Hale to be hanged the next morning.

Hale stayed calm. He spoke to the crowd before he was hanged. His last words were, "I only regret that I have but one life to lose for my country." This is the only part of his speech that we know about. A British officer wrote it down. Hale's last words are still remembered today. They have made Nathan Hale one of the heroes of the American Revolution.

It's a Fact

Nathan Hale didn't think up his last words. He borrowed them from a play written by a British writer.

James Armistead

Hundreds of black people joined the Patriots. One was 22-year-old James Armistead, a slave from Virginia.

Patriot general Lafayette (la-fee-ET) was looking for new soldiers. Armistead convinced his master to let him serve. Armistead got the job of spying on the British.

Armistead was not the usual spy. He was a **double agent**. He pretended to make friends with the British.

James Armistead let the British think he was spying on the Patriots.

Armistead went to the British camp as a laborer. British general Charles Cornwallis (korn-WAH-lis) liked him. He told Armistead that the British would free him from slavery if he spied on the Patriots.

BLACK PATRIOTS IN THE REVOLUTION

One of the first Patriots to die for liberty was Crispus Attucks (KRIS-pus AT-uhks). British soldiers killed him during the Boston Massacre in March 1770. When the war began, only freed black people could serve in the army. Many masters didn't want to lose their slaves in the fighting. Later, the Patriots needed every man they could get. Then slaves were allowed to serve. Some masters said they would free their slaves after the war if the slaves served as soldiers.

Armistead pretended to spy for Cornwallis. All the time he was really spying for the Patriots.

The Patriots used Armistead's information. It helped them defeat Cornwallis at Yorktown in October 1781. Yorktown was the last major battle of the Revolution.

After the battle of Yorktown, Cornwallis went to Patriot headquarters. He was surprised to see the man he thought was his spy. He learned that Armistead had all along been spying on him.

Armistead won his freedom after the war. He spent the rest of his life as a farmer.

1. About 300,000 troops served in the Continental army at one time or another during the Revolution. About 5,000 of them were black. What fraction of all Patriot soldiers were black?

Deborah Samson

Women played an important part in the war. They took care of the homes and families when their husbands went off to fight. They made supplies. They took care of the sick and wounded. A few women fought as soldiers.

One of these brave women was Deborah Samson. Samson was born in Massachusetts. Her father left the family when she was young. Her mother couldn't afford to care for the children. They had to live with different relatives and neighbors.

Deborah worked for a family as a servant for years. Then, in 1782, she got a job as a schoolteacher.

The war was still going on and Deborah wanted to help in the fight. Women were not allowed to be in the army. So, she dressed up as a man. She signed up to be a soldier. She called herself Robert Shurtleff (SHURT-lihf).

Deborah fooled everyone. It helped that she was tall and strong. She was a brave soldier.

Deborah Samson wanted to fight, but women weren't allowed in the army.

One day Deborah was wounded in the leg. She knew if she went to a hospital that doctors might find out she was a woman. So she treated her wound herself and told no one. But the leg never healed right. A short time later she caught a fever. She had to go to the hospital.

A doctor examined her and found out her secret. Deborah was let go from the army in October 1783. Robert Shurtleff was again Deborah Samson.

She went home and married a farmer. They had three children. Deborah also taught school. Nine years after the war, the government gave her money for being a soldier. Deborah Samson was recognized for being as brave as any man.

It's a Fact

Deborah Samson never forgot her days as a soldier. When she was forty-two, she traveled across New England. She gave talks to people about her life as a soldier. She always wore her old uniform when she spoke.

Deborah Samson returned to a normal life as a woman after her military service. ▶

COLONIAL MILITARY LEADERS

George Washington

The Patriots probably would not have won the Revolution without George Washington. He lost many battles. But he knew that if he could keep ahead of the British, he could eventually win. And that's exactly what happened.

Washington grew up on a large farm called a plantation (plan-TAY-shuhn) in Virginia. His family had lived there for more than 100 years. As a boy, George liked the outdoors. He also liked to write poetry.

Washington became a surveyor (ser-VAY-uhr), a person who measures land and marks boundaries. But he really wanted a military career. By age twenty, he was a major in the colonial army.

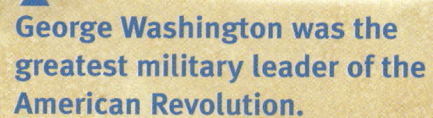

▲ George Washington was the greatest military leader of the American Revolution.

▲ This is a painting of Mount Vernon, George Washington's home.

In 1756, Great Britain and France went to war to get control of North America. This war was called the French and Indian War. Some Native American tribes fought with the French against the British. Young Washington fought on the British side. The British had more men and weapons than the French. They won the war.

After the war, Washington went home to Virginia. He married and became a gentleman farmer. That means other people worked the land for him. He served his community as a judge and a lawmaker.

The British wanted the colonies to help pay for the French and Indian War. They created new taxes that many colonists called unfair.

Colonies met to deal with the problem. They formed the First **Continental Congress** (KAHN-tuh-NEN-tul KAHN-grus)—a formal meeting of government representatives from the colonies.

When the American Revolution began, they chose Washington to lead the new Continental army.

▲ **This famous painting, called "Washington Crossing the Delaware," was made in 1851.**

The Continental army was mostly people with little fighting experience. They **enlisted** for a short term of service. When that time was up, many went home. Sometimes, they left in the middle of battle.

How did Washington keep enough soldiers to fight the British? He would often plan his battles before the soldiers' terms ran out.

The army was always short on clothing and guns. Washington asked the Continental Congress for more supplies. The Congress often ignored his requests.

Washington did the best he could with what he had. The British army was bigger. It was also slower. And Washington was good at fast escapes.

Washington seemed to know the best time to attack the enemy. A good example of this was the Battle of Trenton, New Jersey. Trenton was held by German soldiers hired by the British. On Christmas Day, 1776, the German soldiers were celebrating. Washington decided on a surprise attack.

That night, Washington's soldiers crossed the icy Delaware River in boats. At daybreak, they took the German soldiers by surprise. Washington and his troops moved on and beat the British at nearby Princeton.

There were still tough times ahead and many defeats for Washington's army. But he never gave up.

Washington got help from people in other countries. They shaped up his troops. By spring 1778, Washington's troops fought with great skill. The Patriots went on to win the war. Peace was declared.

They Made a Difference

Thaddeus Kosciuszko

Thaddeus Kosciuszko (THAD-ee-uhs kawsh-CHUSH-koh) was an army engineer (EN-juh-NEER) from the country of Poland. He came to the colonies in 1776. Kosciuzsko built forts and walls to protect Patriots while they were fighting. For his work, Washington made him a general in the Continental army. After the war, Kosciuszko returned to Poland. Years later, when he died, he left instructions that the land he owned in America be sold. He wanted the money to be used to buy freedom for slaves. Kosciuszko was a man who wanted freedom for all people.

Kosciuszko was a Polish army ▶ engineer who helped the Patriots.

13

John Paul Jones

George Washington is called the "Father of our Country." John Paul Jones is called the "Father of the American Navy." He earned this title during the American Revolution.

He was born John Paul in Scotland in 1747. He first went to sea when he was twelve. By age twenty-one, he was commander, or leader, of a ship.

John Paul came to the colonies in 1773. That's when he added "Jones" to his name. When war broke out, he was made a captain in the small Continental navy. Jones sank or captured sixteen British ships in just six weeks.

One day in September 1779, Jones was sailing off the British coast. Suddenly his ship met up with a British warship.

It's a Fact

Captain John Paul Jones named his ship *Bon Homme Richard* (Poor Richard) in honor of Benjamin Franklin's book, *Poor Richard's Almanac.*

"I have not yet begun to fight."

– John Paul Jones

The British ship was bigger and much better armed. The captain asked Jones if he was ready to give up. "Sir," Jones replied, "I have not yet begun to fight."

Jones had his crew tie their ship to the British ship. The two crews fought hand-to-hand for more than two hours. Finally, the Patriots took over the British ship. It was one of the greatest naval victories of the American Revolution.

The war ended, and the Continental navy ended as well. Jones was out of a job.

The queen of Russia hired him to help her fight a war. After that, he settled in Paris, France. He died there in 1792.

Jones's body was brought back to the United States in 1913. His tomb is on display at the Naval Academy in Maryland.

THE CONTINENTAL NAVY

When the Revolution started, the colonies had no navy. The Continental navy's first ships were merchant ships that usually carried trade goods. These ships all ran aground or were captured within a year. Only strong captains like John Paul Jones kept the navy going.

Bernardo de Galvez

Bernardo de Galvez (Ber-NAR-do duh GAL-vez) was the governor of Spanish Louisiana. This huge area later became thirteen states.

Spain officially did not take sides in the American Revolution. But Galvez wanted to help the Patriots defeat the British. He sent supplies and weapons to General Washington.

The British found out and got ready to attack. Galvez beat them to it. He raised a small army. He captured three British forts along the Mississippi River.

▲ **Bernardo de Galvez is one of the lesser-known heroes of the American Revolution.**

✔ POINT

Talk About It
What qualities did George Washington, John Paul Jones, and Bernardo de Galvez share that made them great military leaders? Share your thoughts with a classmate.

By 1781, Galvez had taken over the Mississippi Valley. Next he turned to the Gulf of Mexico. Galvez attacked and captured British forts at Mobile, Alabama and Pensacola, Florida

After the Revolution, Galvez was made governor of New Spain (Mexico). He died a year later, in 1786.

The American people were grateful to Galvez for his victories over the British. The city of Galveston, Texas, was named in his honor.

▲ Bernardo de Galvez leads Spanish troops to victory over the British in Florida.

BRITISH MILITARY LEADERS

The British military leaders didn't understand the type of war they were fighting. They didn't respect the Patriots' fighting ability. They also made many mistakes.

General John Burgoyne

John Burgoyne (Buhr-GOIN) was a popular British general. His men called him "Gentleman Johnny." He treated his men fairly, and they admired him.

"Gentleman Johnny" had a plan to defeat the Patriots. He would divide the colonies in two by taking New York. To do this, he would lead his troops south from Canada. British

▲ "Gentleman Johnny" was well loved by his troops.

general Howe would bring more troops north from Philadelphia (fil-uh-DEL-fyah). Burgoyne left Canada for New York in June 1777, bringing 7,000 soldiers and Native Americans with him.

Burgoyne and his army were still alone when they reached the New York colony. Meanwhile, a large Patriot force was gathering near Saratoga. Burgoyne twice tried to defeat the Patriot troops there, but he failed. He began to retreat north. But it was too late. Howe never showed up to help. Burgoyne surrendered on October 17, 1777.

The Battle of Saratoga was one of the war's most important battles. It made the French think that the Patriots could win. The French joined the Patriot cause by providing weapons and troops.

The Patriots let Burgoyne go. He returned to Great Britain. Many of the British unfairly blamed him for the defeat. Burgoyne left the army in 1782. He died ten years later.

It's a Fact

Burgoyne wrote plays after leaving the army. A number of his comedies were successful on the stage.

▲ British general Burgoyne surrenders his sword to Patriot general Gates after the battle of Saratoga. It was a turning point in the war.

General William Howe

William Howe (HOW) had served bravely in the French and Indian War. Before the American Revolution, Howe was on the Patriot's side. In the Revolution, he fought against the Patriots. People in Britain said that Howe didn't try very hard to beat the Patriots.

When the American Revolution began, Howe went to Boston. He led the British troops at the Battle of Bunker Hill. Soon after, Howe became leader of all British armies in America. He won the Battle of Long Island. He took over New York City.

THE BATTLE OF BUNKER HILL

The Battle of Bunker Hill was actually fought on top of Breed's Hill. On June 16, 1775, the Patriots took positions there. The next day some 2,500 British troops charged up the hill. Twice they failed to take the hill. Then the Patriots ran out of gunpowder and retreated. Although the British won the battle, they lost about 1,000 men.

General Howe had many ▶ chances to finish off Washington's army but didn't take them.

▲ The Battle of Bunker Hill was the first major battle of the American Revolution.

But then, he made two big mistakes. He didn't capture Washington's weak and hungry troops at Valley Forge. Also, he stayed in Philadelphia. He did not go to Saratoga to join Burgoyne. That helped the Patriots win at Saratoga.

In 1778, Howe resigned from the army. He returned to Britain and lived out his life in poor health.

Solve this

2. At the Battle of Bunker Hill, 1,000 British soldiers were killed or wounded. But the Patriots suffered only about 400 casualties (KASH-oo-uhl-teez). What is the ratio of British casualties to Patriot?

21

Joseph Brant

Many Native Americans stayed out of the war between the British and the Patriots. Most Native Americans sided with the British because the colonists had taken their land. The British promised to give the land back if they won.

One of Britain's greatest **allies** was a Mohawk chief named Joseph Brant. Brant grew up liking the British. He fought with them during the French and Indian War.

A British general became Brant's friend. He sent Brant to a school for Native Americans. There, Brant became a Christian. Soon he was telling the Mohawks about being a Christian.

"I bow to no man... But I will shake your hand."

— Joseph Brant

Mohawk Chief Joseph Brant ▶ fought with the British.

▲ **Joseph Brant and the Mohawks battle the Patriots in New York.**

Brant organized Mohawks and other Native American tribes to fight for the British. When the war ended, Brant was on the losing side. Even so, the British gave him 675,000 acres of land in Canada for his people.

Brant put aside his weapons. He went back to telling people about being a Christian. In times of war and peace, he tried to do the best for his people.

It's a Fact

Joseph Brant was well educated. He translated the Book of Common Prayer and the Gospel of St. Mark from the Bible into Mohawk.

CITIZENS

Not everyone fought the war with a gun. Others fought with words. Some urged their fellow Patriots on to action. Others got people in distant countries to support their cause.

Samuel Adams

Samuel Adams was the cousin of John Adams. John Adams was the Patriot leader who later became the second president of the United States.

Before the American Revolution, Sam Adams spoke against the British and their high taxes. He wrote pamphlets. He helped form a protest group called the Sons of Liberty.

▲ Samuel Adams was one of the first spokesmen for revolution.

It's a Fact

Adams was a failure until he discovered politics. He failed as a merchant, then as a partner in his father's brewery. He failed again as Boston's tax collector.

In December 1773, Adams led the Boston Tea Party. The Sons of Liberty dumped chests of British tea into Boston Harbor. Adams was on Britain's list of "most wanted" Patriots. But he escaped.

Samuel Adams was one of the representatives of the First Continental Congress. He served Massachusetts again at the Second Continental Congress. He pushed strongly for independence.

After the war, Adams was governor of Massachusetts. He served from 1793 to 1797.

THE BOSTON TEA PARTY

In December 1773, tea was the one British product with a heavy tax. Many colonies refused to buy British tea in protest. In Boston, three ships loaded with tea sat in the harbor. One night, sixty Sons of Liberty dressed up as Native Americans. They climbed aboard the ships. They dumped 342 chests of tea into the harbor. People watched and cheered. Other "tea parties" took place in other cities. Women led at least one.

Colonists dump ▶ British tea into Boston Harbor to protest unfair taxes.

Mercy Otis Warren

Mercy Otis Warren was a writer. She attacked Loyalists and the British in her writing. She used words to make people laugh and think at the same time.

As a young woman, Mercy couldn't go to college. College was for men only. Her brother, James Otis, would send her his notes from college for her to study.

Mercy married James Warren, a Patriot leader. The Warrens had a large family. Mercy was busy caring for her children. But she always found time to write. Her writing against the British was printed in pamphlets and sold widely. She made fun of the British and Loyalists in poems and such plays as "The Blockheads."

Mercy Otis Warren was known as the "First Lady of the Revolution."
▼

 POINT

Think About It

Both Samuel Adams and Mercy Otis Warren were against the British. How did their ways differ? Reread pages 24–27.

"The origin of all power is in the people." – Mercy Otis Warren

Mercy Otis Warren spoke out on other issues, such as the rights of women. She also wrote one of the first histories of the American Revolution. Her writing was lively and she knew many of the people she wrote about. Mercy Otis Warren spoke out for what she believed until her death in 1814.

Primary Source

". . . man is born free and possessed of certain . . . rights—that government is instituted for the protection, safety and happiness of the people, and not for the profit, honor, or private interest of any man, family, or class of men—That the origin of all power is in the people . . ."
—Mercy Warren, 1788 pamphlet

◀ Colonial America was a land of readers. Printing presses made it easy to run off cheap copies of books, pamphlets, and newspapers by Mercy Otis Warren and other writers.

"We must all hang together, or assuredly we shall all hang separately.

— Ben Franklin

Benjamin Franklin

Benjamin Franklin played many roles during the American Revolution. He was a printer and writer. He spoke out about political issues and knew how to get people to work for freedom. At the signing of the Declaration of Independence, he said, "We must all hang together, or assuredly we shall all hang separately."

In 1776, at age seventy, Franklin went to Paris, France. His job was to get the French to support the colonies in their war with Britain. The French liked everything about Franklin. They liked his simple dress, his good manners, and his way with words.

Benjamin Franklin ▶ went to France to get French support for the Patriots.

News of the Patriot victory at the Battle of Saratoga reached France. The Patriots had proven that they could beat the British. The French were now ready to listen to Franklin.

The French signed a **pact** (PAKT), or agreement, with the Patriots on February 6, 1778. Franklin helped get French troops, weapons, and supplies to the colonies.

The Patriots finally defeated Great Britain at the Battle of Yorktown in 1781. But final peace was slow to arrive. For a whole year, Franklin and others worked on a peace agreement.

The agreement was called the Treaty of Paris. It recognized the United States as a free nation. By this treaty, the British kept Canada but gave Florida back to Spain.

Franklin was one of the signers of the Treaty of Paris in 1783. He returned home two years later. He helped form a new plan of government, the Constitution of the United States.

The Treaty of Paris was signed on ▲ September 3, 1783. It officially ended the American Revolution.

CONCLUSION

The people of the American Revolution gave their all for liberty. Many, such as Nathan Hale, gave their lives. Most were ordinary people such as Deborah Samson and James Armistead. Some, such as Sam Adams, rose to greatness during the Revolution. Others, including George Washington and Ben Franklin, continued to lead the new nation. Use the time line here to tell what these, and other people, did for the American Revolution.

George Washington was sworn in as the first president of the United States in 1789, at Federal Hall in New York City.

TIME LINE OF THE AMERICAN REVOLUTION

1776—Nathan Hale is hanged by British. Washington captures Trenton.

1770

1775

1773—Samuel Adams leads the Boston Tea Party.

1775—Howe leads British troops at Battle of Bunker Hill.

GLOSSARY

ally   (A-ly) on the same side (page 22)

Continental Congress   (KAHN-tuh-NEN-tul KAHN-grus) a formal meeting of government representatives from the colonies (page 11)

double agent   (DUH-bul AY-junt) someone who pretends to spy for one side while actually spying for the other side (page 6)

enlist   (EHN-lihst) to sign up and join the army (page 12)

Loyalist   (LOY-uh-list) a colonist who sided with the British (page 2)

pact   (PAKT) agreement (page 29)

pamphlet   (PAM-flut) a short paper that often discusses current events or ideas (page 3)

Patriot   (PAY-tree-ut) a colonist who wanted freedom from British rule (page 2)

1778—Joseph Brant leads raids through New York colony.

1782—Deborah Samson joins Continental army.

1783—Benjamin Franklin signs Treaty of Paris.

1779—John Paul Jones defeats a British warship.

1780

1805

1777—Burgoyne is defeated at Battle of Saratoga.

1781—Cornwallis is defeated by Washington at Yorktown.

1805—Mercy Otis Warren publishes history of American Revolution.

31

INDEX

Solve this

Answers
1. **Page 7** **1/60**
2. **Page 21** **5 to 2**